388

LOOKING **BACK**
TRANSPORT

NIGEL FLYNN

Wayland

LOOKING BACK

CLOTHES AND FASHION

FAMILY LIFE

FOOD

HOLIDAYS AND PASTIMES

TRANSPORT

WORK

Series and Book Editor: Rosemary Ashley
Designer: Bruce Low

First published in 1991 by
Wayland (Publishers) Limited
61 Western Road Hove,
East Sussex, BN3 1JD, England

British Library Cataloguing in Publication Data
Nigel Flynn
Transport.
1. Transport history
I. Title II. Series
388.09

ISBN 0–7502–0055–3

Typeset by Nicola Taylor, Wayland
Printed in Italy by G. Canale & C.S.p.A., Turin
Bound in Belgium by Casterman S.A.

CONTENTS

INTRODUCTION   4

1 ROAD TRANSPORT   6

2 PEDAL POWER   13

3 RAILWAYS   15

4 SEA TRANSPORT   19

5 IN THE AIR   24

6 JOURNEY INTO SPACE   28

GLOSSARY   30

IMPORTANT DATES   31

BOOKS TO READ   31

INDEX   32

INTRODUCTION

Imagine a world in which there are no aeroplanes, very few cars, no lorries, or any of the other forms of transport we take for granted. One of the things we would surely notice would be the quietness. No thundering lorries, no noisy motorbikes, no sudden roars of aeroplanes tearing through the skies.

This is how the world was in 1900 – a world in which the horse-drawn vehicle was still the commonest form of transport, and most journeys were made on foot.

The enormous changes that have taken place in transport over the past hundred years have transformed the lives of almost everyone on our planet. Today, buses, trains and underground railways carry millions of people to work every day. Goods are transported around the globe by ships, trains and lorries. We can fly across the world in a matter of hours and can even reach the Moon. For short journeys we have the car, bicycle or moped.

Traffic in a London street in 1914. Children cross the road, unworried about the dangers of speeding vehicles.

In 1903 Wilbur and Orville Wright made the first powered flight.

In 1900 these things would have seemed almost unbelievable. Then, the car was just a rich man's toy; controlled flight seemed a dream of the distant future, and space travel was just a fantasy in the minds of science fiction writers. Even in the 1920s and '30s, the pace of life was still comparatively quiet and slow. Although horse-drawn vehicles were becoming rarer, few people owned cars and even fewer travelled by plane. Most people used trains and buses, and underground trains in the big cities. But since the mid-20th century, huge advances in technology have brought about a revolution in road, rail and air transport.

However, in order to create, maintain and fuel today's transport system, huge amounts of the world's natural resources are needed. And these resources are fast being used up. The cost to the environment, too, is alarming. The fuels we use for our modern methods of transport are polluting the air, land and sea, at terrible cost to ourselves and to future generations. There is an urgent need to develop new and more efficient forms of energy to fuel our methods of transport. These future developments are likely to be as dramatic as any that have taken place in the past.

The launch of Apollo 11 on the first stage of its journey to the Moon in 1969.

1 ROAD TRANSPORT

The first cars were invented in the late nineteenth century. Karl Benz in 1885, and Gottlieb Daimler in 1886, both in Germany, produced the first petrol-driven 'horseless carriages'. At about the same time, automobiles, as they were soon to be known, were being developed in the USA.

In the early years of the century motoring was a privilege enjoyed only by the rich. Cars were expensive, noisy,

'Travelling with an incredible rate of speed, motor-cars scramble and smash and shriek along all the rural ways. You can see the evidence of their activity in the dust-laden hedges of the south country roads, a grey mud colour, with no evidence of green, and in the ruined cottage gardens of the south country villages.'
From *The Condition of England*, by F. Masterman, 1909

Early motorists were seen as mad, bad and dangerous.

The age of elegant motoring: resting by the roadside, 1922.

uncomfortable, and by today's standards, very slow. Cars were open-topped and motorists were exposed in all weathers. They froze in winter and in summer were covered in dust thrown up from the poor road surface. Many people thought of motoring as a dangerous sport rather than as a means of transport. The noisy arrival of cars in the peaceful countryside upset some people so much that they scattered broken glass and tacks on the road to try to keep them away!

In the USA, in 1908, Henry Ford produced his famous Model T Ford. His idea was to make the motor car affordable to large numbers of people. Motor companies in Europe soon followed his example, and by the 1920s, mass-produced 'family tourers' such as the 'Tin Lizzie' – as the Model T Ford was nicknamed – and the 'Baby' Austin were being driven by millions. These cars were rarely used for business, but were kept for family 'joy-rides' into the countryside or to the seaside at

By 1939 there were filling stations for private motorists all over Britain.

weekends. In Britain, the official speed limit of 20 miles per hour was largely ignored, and with no driving test, no highway code, and driving licences available to anyone over the age of 16, the number of road accidents became, in the words of a government minister, 'a hideous growing blot on national life'. Even in 1939, only one family in ten in Britain owned a car, and for most people, road transport meant travelling by bus or tram.

After the Second World War (1939–45), the appearance of cars changed dramatically. In the USA their size and design grew larger and ever more spectacular. In Europe, however, the high price of fuel and congested traffic conditions encouraged the development of small, light-weight cars.

By the middle of the century cars had greatly improved technically. Greater engine power meant that they were faster than ever before, while improved tyres gave better road-holding and disc brakes, power-assisted steering, wrap-around windscreens – all American inventions – made driving safer and more comfortable.

In the second half of the century, to cope with the ever-increasing number of cars, motorways were hastily built. But they seemed unable to solve the problem of traffic congestion. In cities, traffic jams, air pollution and frayed nerves became a way of life. It is now recognized that fumes from car exhausts are a major source of pollution, and with fears that cars are contributing to the

'Father has bought a car – I'm so excited. I shall call her Sally because she is definitely a lady car. She is a dark-blue Austin, very smart and shiny, and she has comfy, blue leather seats. Father showed me her engine – it's under her 'bonnet' and it's all silvery. When he turned the handle at the front to start her engine, it made a great roar. On Sunday, Father is going to drive us over to visit Aunt Mary in Chiswick. She will get such a surprise to see us arriving like royalty.'

Diary entry of a young girl in 1932

The shape of modern motoring: fast, comfortable and streamlined.

Since Britain's first motorway was built in 1957, a network of motorways has been constructed all over the country.

warming up of the Earth's atmosphere, many are beginning to question whether the motor car was such a wonderful invention after all.

Buses were the usual form of transport for most people living in cities before the 1950s. Getting to work, going out for the evening or taking a holiday, usually meant travelling by bus or coach. The first buses appeared in the early 1900s.

By the 1920s their numbers had grown dramatically. Most had no fixed routes or even regular stops. In the big cities, buses on the busiest routes ran every one or two minutes. In country regions the open-topped charabanc, crowded with day-trippers, was a familiar sight at weekends.

Despite the huge increase in private motoring in the second half of the century, the bus is

> *'I sought out US 90... a multiple-lane carrier of the nation's goods... Trucks as long as freighters went roaring by, delivering a wind like the blow of a fist. These great roads are wonderful for moving goods but not for inspection of a countryside. You are bound to the wheel and your eyes to the car ahead and to the rear-view mirror... at the same time you must read all the signs for fear you miss instructions...When we get these thruways across the whole country, as we will and must, it will be possible to drive from New York to California without seeing a single thing.'*
> From *Travels With Charlie* by John Steinbeck, 1962

still the main form of transport for millions of people throughout the world.

Trams still run in many cities throughout the world, although in Britain they have not been used since 1962 – almost a hundred years after they first appeared. Trams ran on rails and were originally horse-drawn, but by the 1930s they were driven by electric motors powered through overhead cables. Although popular because they were very cheap, trams were restricted to routes where there were rails. Because they could not pull into the kerb, passengers had to get on and off in the middle of the road, and risked being knocked down by other traffic.

A sight-seeing tour in a charabanc in the 1920s.

Passengers waiting to board a trolleybus in a London suburb in the 1930s. You can see the overhead electric cables that powered trolley buses.

Trolleybuses were introduced in the 1930s. They looked very much like buses. Their only difference was that they were powered by electricity, which was supplied through overhead cables. The need for these cables restricted the use of trolleybuses, and although they were quieter and cleaner than both trams and buses, they were withdrawn in Britain, after only twenty years of service.

'One private bus made a point of never leaving anyone behind, however full the bus. Sometimes there were many more standing than sitting; or there would be four to a seat, girls sitting on laps... At stops there always seemed to be someone at the very back of the bus wanting to get out. Amid groans from those already squeezed as tight as could be in aisles and yells of dismay as toes were unavoidably trodden on... those nearer the exit piled out, sometimes into pouring rain... [or] pitch dark, to let this one person out.'

A worker describes a rural bus journey in England during the Second World War

2 PEDAL POWER

Bicycles have hardly changed in appearance since the early 1900s, although today they are lighter, safer and faster.
In 1885, the first safety bicycle was produced, with equal-sized wheels, cranks, and pedals mounted between the wheels, and a chain to drive the rear wheel. Air-filled tyres were added in 1890. Cycling was now much smoother than it had been previously, when bicycles known as 'penny-farthings' (with one huge and one small wheel) meant a wobbly ride for long-legged cyclists.

In the years before 1914, cycling in the countryside became a craze with young men and women. At weekends, office and factory workers would cycle through country lanes, away from the smoke and grime of the big cities.

In the early years of the century cycling provided easy transport and was an enjoyable pastime for many people.

During the 1920s and '30s, cycling remained popular, although it had become more dangerous because of the increasing numbers of cars and lorries on the roads. Children usually started riding tricycles and would graduate to the 'fairy cycle', which was a small version of the safety bike. During the Second World War petrol was rationed and there was little private motoring, so cycling became the best way of getting around. Through the 1950s it remained the only form of personal transport available to most people.

In the 1960s, the availability of light-weight motor-bikes, scooters and mopeds meant that cycling became less attractive to many and the number of bicycles sold in Western countries dropped by half. Now the bicycle is becoming popular again. Cycling is often the fastest way to get through crowded city streets. It is a cheap and efficient form of transport, and does not harm the environment.

'I can remember very clearly the journeys I made to and from school because they were so tremendously exciting... The excitement centred around my new tricycle. I rode to school on it every day with my sister riding on hers. No grown-ups came with us... All this, you must realize, was in the good old days when the sight of a motor car on the street was an event, and it was quite safe for tiny children to go tricycling and whooping their way to school in the centre of the highway.'
Roald Dahl, recalling his childhood in Llandaff, Glamorgan, Wales, in 1922 (From *Boy*)

Left *Cycling has become an exciting sport for many children. These boys are practising for a track race.*

3 RAILWAYS

The writer Rudyard Kipling described a typical country station before 1914. 'The train stopped in a blaze of sunshine at Framlyngham Admiral, which is made up entirely of the nameboard, two platforms and an overhead bridge... One could hear the drone of conversation along the carriages and scarcely less loud, the drone of bumble-bees in the wallflowers up the bank.'

At this time no one could have imagined that steam locomotives would have such a short future. Throughout the world they were the principal form of transport for both passengers and goods. Today, in the advanced industrial countries, steam has been replaced by electric or diesel locomotives, and railways themselves have declined with the increase of road transport and aviation.

Steam trains, with their engines streaming plumes of smoke, are still a fond memory for many. They were replaced by electric and diesel engines in the 1960s.

> 'In those days...the trains were steam ones, and there was something awe-inspiring about the snorting, throbbing engines which made the whole station shudder when they drew to the platform. Smoke puffed from the chimney, and steam gushed from various points along the side of the monster. Doors clanged, porters yelled, whistles blew, flags waved – the din was tremendous.'
>
> The London surburban railway in the 1920s. From *Time Remembered* by 'Miss Read'

Even before the First World War (1914–18) a number of countries, notably Italy and Germany, had experimented with electric trains. Compared to steam, electric locomotives are simpler, easier to maintain and do not give off unpleasant fumes. They are also capable of maintaining high speeds over long distances. However, the electrifying of railways on a large scale did not take place until after the Second World War, during which a large number of Europe's railways had been destroyed.

In the years between the wars (1918–39) steam still dominated – as it does today in Eastern Europe, China, India and parts of Africa.

The elegant dining car of a passenger train in the early 1900s.

A busy station in Pakistan. In many developing countries steam trains are an important means of transport.

As an alternative to both steam and electricity, diesel engines were introduced in a number of European countries and the United States in the 1920s and '30s. The advantage of diesel locomotives was that they were cleaner and faster than steam and, because they could run on existing track, they cost less than switching to electric locomotives.

Coping with the millions of people who travel to work every day in big cities is a major problem for transport planners throughout the world. One solution was found in December 1890, when the world's first electrically-operated under-ground train service opened in

' "A terrific gabble... Men with dhotis *running along with things on their heads, men with broken-down umbrellas trying to get on the train. You'd see people clinging on the carriages, even on the roof, and the stationmaster trying to pull them off"... child beggars hung on to carriage windows as the train pulled out, "screeching and looking at us with great spaniel's eyes until you had to tap their knuckles, so that they would drop off all along the platform like little flies".* '

An Englishman recalls travelling on an Indian train in the 1930s.
From *Plain Tales from the Raj* edited by Charles Allen

The Japanese Hikari *or* Bullet *train travels at speeds of up to 250 km/h.*

south London. By moving people on fast trains underground, it was hoped to relieve traffic congestion on the roads. Today, there are underground railways in many cities throughout the world.

A London underground train. Early trains were steam-powered and the tunnels are still sooty from their engines.

'People started to flock towards the tube. They wanted to get underground. Thousands upon thousands of people... pushed their way into Liverpool Street Station... Here was a new life, a whole city under the world. We rode up and down the escalators. The children of London were adapting themselves to the times, inventing new games, playing hopscotch... and I used to ride backwards and forwards in the trains, to see the other stations of underground people.'

A description of London Underground during the Blitz, September 1940, From *The World is a Wedding* by Bernard Kops, 1963

4   SEA TRANSPORT

In the days before jet aircraft, travelling between continents meant a voyage by ship. In the years before 1914, enormous ocean liners from Britain, France and Germany took over five days to cross the Atlantic to North America. They took over three weeks to reach Australia. Some of these great ships, like the *Mauretania* and *Lusitania,* were the last word in comfort and elegance – for those rich enough to pay. For others, including millions of immigrants who made the crossing from Europe to the USA in the first years of the century, conditions were often appalling.

When the 'unsinkable' Titanic sank on its maiden voyage to New York in 1912, 1,502 people were drowned.

'*On September 7, 1907 the* Lusitania *sailed from Liverpool to New York on her maiden voyage; and it is no exaggeration to say that never before had such widespread interest been taken in the first sailing of any liner. Fully 200,000 people witnessed her departure... The cheering of the vast crowds, supplemented by the steam whistles of all the shipping on the river at the time... made this epoch-making event a memorable one... Her reception on the other side of the Atlantic was just as hearty, a whole fleet of tugs and pleasure steamers greeting her as she entered the newly-dredged Ambrose Channel.*'

From a booklet about the *Lusitania*, published by the Cunard Company, October 1915

These huge ships were powered by steam and more than 1,000 tonnes of coal a day were needed to fuel them. But by the late 1920s and '30s a new generation of oil-fuelled liners had arrived; bigger, faster and even more luxurious than the earlier ships.

The luxurious accommodation of an ocean liner in the 1930s.

With the coming of war in 1939, many British liners were used as troopships. They were also used to transport children from Britain to the safety of Canada and the USA.

On the day the Second World War began, 3 September 1939, the liner *Athenia*, carrying hundreds of women and children bound for Montreal, Canada, was sunk by a German U-boat off the coast of Ireland.

Giant liners in dock. Ship-building and re-fitting provided work for thousands.

After the war, fewer people travelled by sea, a trend that had already begun before the war. With fast, cheap air travel now available to all, the day of the big ocean liner was over.

'We were sitting on a hatch feeling sick when we were blown up into the air. I wasn't hurt but mother hurt her shoulder. After we were blown in the air we were put in a lifeboat. I climbed into it myself. Then we were out on the ocean all night. Nobody said much, and there was no singing or laughing or crying. We saw a battleship and climbed on to it up a ladder. The sailors were very kind and we were taken to Greenock in Scotland. Mother was in hospital... but I was up and around.'

Rosie Ralph, aged 10.
From *Children of the Blitz*,
by Robert Westall, 1983

Although massive, prestigious liners such as the QE2 (launched in 1967) continued to be built, they were, and still are, used mainly by wealthy people for luxury holiday cruises.

Ships have always been used to transport goods to and from different parts of the world. Cargo ships have changed a great deal since the turn of the century, when coal-fired tramp steamers plied the oceans of the world, carrying cargoes of food and other commodities. Today, huge supertankers carry up to half a million tonnes of crude oil in their holds – enough to power all the motor vehicles of a country the size of Britain for a week.

'I was a cabin boy and often worked fourteen hours a day and Sunday was like a Monday, in fact Sunday was worse because it was Captain's inspection day, 9.0 a.m. sharp. If everything was not in order you were "logged" 5 shillings loss of pay. Then there were the "field days" that we hated, when all hands were ordered out to work extra to their normal watch, usually chipping and painting. It was very rarely that there was any overtime pay and if you complained you were never employed by that company again.'
S.Banda, SS *Zouave*, describing life on a merchantman in the 1930s. From *Convoy*, 1978

The QE2 in New York. Today's ocean liners provide luxury cruises for the very rich.

Before the Second World War, Britain had the largest number of merchant ships in the world. However, by the 1930s, the fleet was becoming old and dilapidated. During the war, many British ships were sunk by German U-boats. So many ships were lost that Britain's link with vital supplies from overseas was almost destroyed.

Since 1945, merchant ships have grown bigger and are now among the largest man-made structures on Earth. Bulk goods, such as oil, grain and iron ore, are carried in these enormous craft, and manufactured goods are carried in standard-sized boxes called containers, which are easy to load and unload. For short sea crossings, roll-on-roll-off ferries are used. Lorries loaded with freight drive on to the ferry, are taken across the water, and drive off to continue their road journey on the other side.

On 25 July 1959 a strange-looking craft, powered by a single diesel engine, crossed the English Channel at a rate of 25 knots, hovering just 23 cm above the surface of the sea. Called a hovercraft, it was hailed as 'travelling's biggest break-through since the wheel'.

Some supertankers have decks so long that their crew use bicycles to get from one end to the other.

The hovercraft floats on a cushion of air and can travel over land and sea.

Because the hull of a conventional ship is always partly under water, friction between the hull and the water reduces its speed. By pumping air round the outside of the hull to form an air-cushion, the hovercraft is lifted above the surface, enabling it to overcome friction and so attain greater speed. Shortly after the hovercraft's maiden 'flight', a flexible 'skirt' was placed all round the base of the craft to completely trap the air-cushion. The result was that the hovercraft was found to rise 1.2 m, high enough to clear any normal-sized wave. And when fitted with a jet engine in place of the original diesel, the craft was able to skim over land and sea at a speed of 55 knots.

The hydrofoil, which was first developed in Germany in 1936, is similar to the hovercraft. Hydrofoils skim across water on skis and can reach speeds of up to 110 km/h. The high speeds of both hydrofoils and hovercraft mean that they are useful for transporting passengers on short sea crossings.

5   IN THE AIR

The monoplane flown by Louis Blériot on the first flight across the English Channel in 1909.

For more than two thousand years, since the days of the Ancient Greeks, humans have wanted to fly. On 17 December 1903, two brothers, Wilbur and Orville Wright, became the first men to do so in a powered, controlled aircraft. Taking off in their primitive biplane from Kitty Hawk, on the coast of North Carolina, USA, they flew for 12 seconds. Few people at the time realized that this short flight would change transport throughout the world. One who did, Robert Baden-Powell (founder of the Scouting movement), said 'The Wrights are in possession of a power which controls the fate of nations.'

Others were less far-sighted. When the Frenchman Louis Blériot crossed the English Channel in a monoplane in 1909, a journalist wrote that aeroplanes 'represent a foolish waste of money'. Despite Orville Wright's hope that the aeroplane 'would make further wars practically impossible', the use of aircraft as a weapon of war was soon recognized. By 1918, at the end of the First World War, both Britain and Germany possessed aircraft capable of carrying bombs to each other's homeland. Planes were faster, more manoeuvrable, and could fly higher and for longer periods, than would have been thought possible only four years before.

By 1939, improvements in design had resulted in much faster aircraft, and distant parts of the world now seemed to have been brought much closer.

'The first aeroplane I actually saw was one I watched through the nursery window above the school playing-fields. Suddenly it nose-dived. I heard later that the pilot was an old boy of the school. His younger brother was on the playing field, he knew his brother was in the plane, and he saw it crash... Often since then watching planes cross the sky, I half-expect to see them fall to earth, as though it were my gaze which had caused that first crash.'

Graham Greene recalling an incident when he was seven years old.
From *A Sort of Life*, 1971

Fighter planes of the 1914–18 war were built of wood covered with fabric. There was little protection for the pilots.

The Atlantic was first flown in 1919 by John Alcock and Arthur Whitten Brown, in 16 hours 27 minutes, and in 1933 Wiley Post made the first round-the-world flight in 7 days, 18 hours and 49 minutes. In the years before the Second World War, only a small number of passengers flew between continents, with frequent stops for refuelling.

In 1939, a German plane, the Heinkel HE 178, rose into the air to make the first successful jet-powered flight. The jet engine was to completely change military and civilian aviation. The world's first jet passenger service started in 1952, with the

Flying boats were a popular form of air transport in the 1930s. They took off and landed on water.

'When I left home in my youth it took me two years of foot-slogging and scheming to get from Gloucestershire to the north of Spain. The other day I travelled practically the whole of that distance – and back – in one hour and forty-five minutes... in Concorde. There is no doubt that the Concorde is a magnificent contrivance – you can leave in daylight for New York and arrive to find it waiting for sunrise. The device is fantastic; it could telescope the world. It could also diminish our sense of distance and wonder.'

From *I Can't Stay Long*
by Laurie Lee, 1975

Soaring to the fringes of space, Concorde can reach a speed of 2,100 km/h.

De Havilland *Comet* flying between London and Johannesburg, South Africa, and by the 1970s bigger and faster jets were carrying millions of passengers all over the world. In 1971, passengers aboard *Concorde*, the world's first supersonic passenger aircraft, zipped across the Atlantic in a mere 3 hours 50 minutes.

Helicopters are aircraft that can hover and move vertically as well as horizontally. Drawings by Leonardo da Vinci, in the 15th century, show that the idea of the helicopter is older even than that of the aeroplane. But it was not until the 1920s that the first one took to the air. In 1930 an Italian helicopter stayed in the air for just under nine minutes.

In 1939, Igor Sikorsky successfully tested his VS-300 in the USA. It had a single lifting rotor and a stabilizing propeller mounted sideways at the end of the fuselage. In 1944 he produced the first practical helicopter to be used for transport. Since then helicopters have become a familiar sight all over the world. The fact that they can fly forward and backward, hang motionless in the air and take-off and land vertically, makes them an invaluable means of transport, with many uses.

Helicopters are used to carry soldiers to the heart of a battle zone.

6 JOURNEY INTO SPACE

The story of our journey into space has only recently begun. In 1944, German V-2 rockets carrying explosive warheads soared 60 miles above Earth, before plummeting down on their target. After the war, German scientists and technology were used by both the USA and USSR to build their own defensive rockets. By the 1950s both countries had rockets capable of carrying deadly weapons 600 miles into space before

'I remember the Moon landing clearly because my father woke me up in the middle of the night. He said that it was an historic event and that I should watch it. Before I went back to bed, I looked at the Moon through my bedroom window. It seemed odd to think that as I was looking at it men were actually walking on its surface, and that I had seen them on television. Since than I have never been able to look at the Moon in quite the same way as before. It had lost its strangeness and mystery'
An English schoolgirl, 1980.

descending on each other's territory. It was these rockets that were adapted to launch the first men into space.

On 12 April 1961, the Soviet cosmonaut Yuri Gagarin became the first man to travel in space. In his spaceship Vostok I, he orbited the Earth in 1 hour 48 minutes, before re-entering the Earth's atmosphere.

Left *The most powerful rocket ever built, the* Saturn V, *burns 15 tonnes of fuel per second at lift-off.*

American astronaut 'Buzz' Aldrin walking on the moon, 20 July 1969.

On 21 July 1969 Neil Armstrong, an American astronaut, watched by millions of people on their TV sets on Earth, stepped from his Apollo spacecraft on to the surface of the Moon. It was, he said, 'one small step for a man, one giant leap for mankind'.

Since Armstrong's historic space voyage, there have been many other space journeys. Unmanned spacecraft have landed on Mars and have sent back pictures of this inhospitable planet. *Voyager* spacecraft have sent back pictures of the outermost planets in our solar system, on their way far out into deepest space.

Space flight has been an enormous achievement of the twentieth century. In the sixty-six years between the Wright Brothers' 12-second flight in 1903, to Neil Armstrong's historic moon landing in 1969, humans have progressed, technically, faster than in their previous million years of existence. Not only have the principles of flight been mastered, but those of space travel as well.

The Space Shuttle takes off like a rocket and lands like a plane.

GLOSSARY

Aviation The art or science of flying aircraft.

Biplane An aeroplane with two sets of wings, one above the other.

Charabanc An open-topped motor coach.

Commodities Manufactured items.

Dhoti A loin cloth worn by men in India.

Disc brakes Disc-shaped pads which press against the wheels of a car on each side when the brakes are operated.

Freight Goods transported by land, sea and air.

Freighters Ships or aircraft that carry cargo.

Fuselage The body of an aeroplane.

Horseless carriage The original name given to the motor car.

Immigrants People who move into a foreign country and settle there.

Jet engine An engine that works by air being sucked in at the front and put under pressure. Fuel is sprayed into the compressed air to make a mixture which burns fiercely. The hot gases which rush to escape from the engine's tailpipe provide the thrust to drive the aircraft forward.

Knot The measurement of speed equivalent to one nautical mile an hour.

Maiden flight The first flight of an aircraft.

Manoeuvrable The ability to turn and move easily.

Monoplane An aeroplane with a single set of wings.

Motorways Roads with four or more lanes, specially built for fast motor traffic.

Penny-farthing An old type of bicycle, popular in the nineteenth century. So-called because its two wheels resembled the large bronze penny coin and small farthing coin of British currency.

Ration A fixed amount of food.

Rotor The horizontally rotating blade of a helicopter.

Supersonic Faster than the speed of sound. At sea level this is 1,220 km/h, but it slows down in the cold air higher up.

Tramp steamer A merchant ship that does not run between ports on a regular schedule but carries cargo wherever the shippers desire.

U-boat A German submarine.

PICTURE ACKNOWLEDGEMENTS
The publishers wish to thank the following for providing the photographs in this book: Mary Evans Picture Library cover, 5 (top), 6, 7, 16, 19; Eye Ubiquitous 17, Billie Love 4, 8, 11, 20, (lower), Mansell Collection 13; Peter Newark's Pictures 5 (lower), 18 (top), 27, 28, 29 (both); Topham Photo Library 20 (top), 26 (lower); Wayland Picture Library 9, 10, 12, 14, 15, 18, (lower), 21, 22, 23, 24, 25, 26, (top).

IMPORTANT DATES

1901 Queen Victoria's death. King Edward VII comes to the throne.

1903 Wilbur and Orville Wright make the first powered, controlled flight, lasting 12 seconds.

1908 Model T Ford first produced. Wilbur Wright makes flight lasting 30 mins.

1914–18 First World War.

1919 John Alcock and Arthur Whitton Brown make first non-stop transatlantic flight from Newfoundland to Ireland.

1935 Pedestrian crossings and 30 mph speed limit in built-up areas introduced.

1939 First jet aircraft flew in Germany.
Igor Silorsky made first serviceable helicopter.

1952 First flight of *Comet* jet passenger aircraft.

1958 Sputnik III launched by USSR.

1959 Invention of the hovercraft.

1961 Yuri Gagarin orbited the Earth in space capsule.

1969 First moon landing. Concorde made first flight.

1976 *Viking* spacecraft launched.

1981 Space shuttle launched.

1989 *Galileo* space probe launched to reach Jupiter 1995.

BOOKS TO READ

General books on transport

Colour Book of Transport, The by Robert Welsh (Octopus, 1982)

Land and Sea Transport by Hugh Johnstone (Gloucester Press, 1989)

Transport by Nick Hamer (Franklin Watts, 1982)

Transport and Travel from the 1930s to the 1980s by Francis Wilkins (Batsford, 1985)

Individual forms of transport

Airliner by Nigel Cawthorne (Gloucester Press, 1987)

Helicopters by Charles Messenger (Franklin Watts, 1985)

Our Future in Space by Tim Furniss (Wayland, 1985)

Railways: A history in photographs, 1850s to the present day by Penny Marshall (Macdonald, 1985)

ACKNOWLEDGEMENTS

Quotations on the following pages are reprinted by kind permission of; Jonathan Cape Ltd., from *Boy* by Roald Dahl page 14, Michael Joseph Ltd., from *Time Remembered* by 'Miss Reed' page 16, Vallentine Mitchell from *The World is a Wedding* by Bernard Kops page 18, The Bodley Head from *A Sort of Life* by Graham Greene page 25, André Deutsch Ltd., from *I Can't Stay Long* by Laurie Lee page 26.

INDEX

aeroplanes 4, 5, 24–7
Aldrin, Edwin 'Buzz' 29
Alcock, John 25
Apollo spacecraft 5, 29
Armstrong, Neil 29
astronaut 29
Athenia 20

'Baby Austin' 7, 8
Benz, Karl 6
bicycles 13–14
Blériot, Louis 24
Brown, Arthur Whitton 25
buses 5, 10–11

Canada 20
cars 4, 5, 6–12
charabancs 11
coaches 10
Comet 27
Concorde 26, 27
Cosmonaut 28

Daimler, Gottlieb 6
diesel locomotives 5, 8
disk brakes 9
driving licences 8

electric locomotives 15, 17
engine power 8

ferries 22, 23
fighter planes 25
filling stations 8
First World War 25
flying boats 26
Ford, Henry 7
fuel 5, 8

Gagarin, Yuri 28

Heinkel HE 17, 25
helicopters 27
highway code 8
Hikari Express (Bullet train 17, 18)
horse-drawn vehicles 4, 5
'horseless carriages' 6
hovercraft 22, 23
hydrofoil 23

immigrants 19
India 16, 17

Japan 17, 18
jet aircraft 19
jet engine 25

liners 19, 20, 21
lorries 4, 22
Lusitania 19

Mauretania 19
merchant ships 21, 22
Model T Ford 7
mopeds 14
motorbikes 4, 14
motorists 6
motorways 9, 10

petrol rationing 14
petrol station 8
pollution 5, 9
Post, Wiley 25
power assisted brakes 9

QE2 21

railways 15–18
railway station 15, 16
road accidents 8
roads 7, 8, 11

Saturn V 28
scooters 14
Second World War 8, 14, 16, 20, 22, 25
ships 4, 19–23
Sikorsky, Igor 27
Space Shuttle 29
space travel 28–9
speed limit 8
steam trains 15, 17
supertanker 21, 22

technology 5, 28
Titanic 19
traffic congestion 8, 9
trains 5, 15–18
trams 11–12
trolleybuses 12
troopships 20

U-boats 20, 22
underground trains 4, 5, 17–18
USA 6, 8, 17, 28
USSR 28

V-2 rockets 28
Vinci, Leonardo da 27
Vostock 1 28
Voyager spacecraft 29

Wright, Orville and Wilbur 5, 24, 29